THIRTY TRUTHS
for Common Lies

{FOR TEENS}

ALEXA HESS

WHEN THE ENEMY
WHISPERS LIES
TO US, WE CAN
COMBAT THEM
WITH THE TRUTH
OF GOD'S WORD.

TABLE OF *Contents*

Introduction

Many people have a running narrative in their minds. As we go throughout our day-to-day lives, we think about what we are going to eat next, how well we did on a recent test, or our upcoming weekend plans. However, many of us also have moments in our everyday lives when a lie pierces our minds. *You aren't good enough. You don't matter. Other people are more liked than you.* Often, but not always, certain events will trigger these lies. When we mess up on a test, someone says something mean to us, or we forget to do what our parents ask, these thoughts can enter in without our permission. Or perhaps other people have spoken lies to us. They are the ones who tell us, "You are not good enough," "You don't matter," or "Other people are more liked than you." When we dwell on lies, whether spoken to us or existing within our minds, we can start to believe these words are true. If we accept these lies rather than fight against them, we can find our self-worth crushed, our faith tested, and our purpose questioned.

Why do we believe lies? Why is it so easy to buy into the words that enter our minds or are spoken to us? We believe lies because of sin. When God created the world, He proclaimed all of creation good. Not one part of God's creation was imperfect or evil. Humans experienced what it was like to walk with God and live with minds and bodies that were at peace. While Adam and Eve were free to eat from any tree in the garden, they were not allowed to eat from the Tree of Knowledge of Good and Evil. As long as Adam and Eve obeyed this command, they would continue to delight in the abundance of both creation and the Creator.

But one day, Satan took the form of a serpent and approached Eve. Satan questioned God's command to Adam and Eve and even refuted God's words. Satan told Eve, "No! You will certainly not die. ... In fact, God knows that when you eat it your eyes will be opened and you will be like God, knowing good and evil" (Genesis 3:4–5). Satan tempted Eve not only to doubt God's command but also to believe that God was withholding good from her by His command. Sadly, Eve believed the lie of the serpent and ate the fruit. Adam, too, took the fruit and ate it, and through their disobedience, sin entered the world.

Sin clouds our judgment and causes us to believe the deceiver rather than the God of truth. Without a relationship with God, our eyes are blinded, and our ears are blocked from receiving truth. On our own, we are defenseless to rid ourselves of the sin that entangles us and come back to the God we deny. But, out of His abundant grace and mercy, God sent us Jesus, who is full of grace and truth (John 1:14). Jesus took the punishment we deserve for our sin by dying on the cross; three days later, Jesus rose from the dead, declaring His power over sin and death.

When we repent of our sin and trust in Jesus, we receive forgiveness for our sin. The grace of Jesus opens our eyes and ears, uniting us with the God of truth. Through God's Word, we are able to be people who walk in truth and lead others to the truth of the gospel. However, while we have a redeemed heart, we still have a sinful nature and a very present enemy. Daily, we will battle against the lies Satan places in our minds. But we do not have to succumb to these lies of the enemy or the lies of sinful mankind. As followers of Christ, we have the Holy Spirit inside us who helps us fight against lies. Through the power of the Spirit, we are able to resist the father of lies and rest in our heavenly Father, who speaks truth over us. As believers, we have not only the Spirit but also God's Word. When the enemy whispers lies to us, we can combat them with the truth of God's Word.

In this booklet, we will walk through thirty everyday lies we often hear or maybe even tell ourselves. We will tackle each lie with the truth of Scripture and be reminded of what is true in Christ. We will learn how to speak truth over ourselves when lies invade and recognize habits of thought that cause us to be deceived. Most of all, we will learn how, through the power of God's Word, we can fight against everyday lies and rest in the God of truth.

Editors' Note: This booklet was written with the intent of helping you apply biblical truth to lies you may believe. Some of these lies may apply to you, and some may not, based on where you live, your culture, your personal struggles, or any number of factors. However, through this resource, we hope you will find truth to combat whatever lies are impacting you.

TIPS FOR
Combating Lies

BE IN GOD'S WORD DAILY

We need to regularly be in God's Word to know God's truth. If we remove ourselves from God's Word, we leave ourselves vulnerable in the moments lies strike. Without the regular reminder of the truths of God's Word, we can easily buy into the lies we hear and see. Make it a priority to be in God's Word daily so that you can learn what is true and rest in what is true.

MEMORIZE SCRIPTURE

Along with regularly reading God's Word, we can memorize what God's Word says. Memorizing Scripture helps us call to mind God's truth when lies arise. You can combat lies by speaking these memorized truths over yourself. You can choose something to memorize from your personal Bible reading or consider selecting some of the verses listed in this booklet to memorize. Here are three methods for memorization:

1. Say the verse aloud, and repeat each part several times.

2. Write out the verse over and over on a piece of paper.

3. Follow the letter method by writing the first letter of every word to the verse and memorizing the word that accompanies that letter. For example, you would write out T T I N N C F T I C J to help you memorize "Therefore, there is now no condemnation for those in Christ Jesus" (Romans 8:1).

3 PRAY

When lies strike, you can ask the Lord to remind you of His truth. You can ask for His voice to be louder than the lies and for God to help you cling to what is true. You can also ask God to give you the discernment to know whether something is true or not. It can be hard at times to know if something you read or see is true, but you can ask God to give you the wisdom to distinguish between lies and truth.

4 SHARE WITH OTHERS

God has given us our fellow believers to help shoulder our burdens. If you are struggling with certain lies, share this struggle with a trusted friend, pastor, or counselor. Talking through lies you are wrestling with allows others to speak truth into your life. Sharing your struggles with a community also allows other brothers and sisters to point out lies that you perhaps weren't even aware you were believing.

01

Lie:

I am not pretty or good-looking enough

No matter the flaws we perceive in ourselves, we are wonderfully made by God.

The girl on social media who seems to be in better shape than you. The classmate with the hair you so desperately wish you had. The model with perfect skin in the advertisement that popped up on your screen. We can look at all these people and compare them to the person we see in the mirror, disliking who and what we see.

The word "enough" signifies a comparison between ourselves and something or someone else. When we say that we are not pretty or good-looking enough, we are saying that our looks do not measure up to another's. We then might criticize how we were made or try all that we can to look like the person whose image we crave. But comparison does us more harm than good. While some instances of comparison can help us see important changes we need to make in our lives, comparison, more often than not, makes us feel insecure. The more we compare ourselves to others, the more bitter we can become toward ourselves, others, and maybe even God.

In Psalm 139:14, David prays these profound words to God: "I will praise you because I have been remarkably and wondrously made." No matter the flaws we perceive in ourselves, we are wonder-fully made by God. This means the shape of our noses, the color of our skin, and the size of our feet have all been craft-ed by the hands of an intentional and holy God. To criticize how we look is to criticize the handiwork of a God who knew exactly what He was doing when He created us. We can love the size of our bodies, the texture or color of our hair, or the freckles on our skin, knowing that our heavenly Father designed us with these qualities. If a perfect and holy God cannot make mistakes, then how He created us is sure-ly not a mistake.

Instead of comparing ourselves to others, we need to view ourselves through the lens of the God who made us. We need to look in the mirror through His eyes, marveling at the work of creation that stares back at us. When we cel-ebrate rather than criticize how God made us, we will not be as inclined to compare ourselves to others. We will not become bitter toward those we wish we looked like, but instead, we will celebrate how God uniquely made them as well.

WHO WE ARE IS A REFLECTION OF THE GOD WHO CREATED US.

In Psalm 139, David praises the Lord for creating him, and so should we. God is worthy to be worshiped as Creator, not only for cre-ating the world around us but also for making us. In fact, when we gaze around at creation, we are reminded that we, too, have been crafted by the same hands that placed the stars in the sky and formed the waves of the ocean. And, when we go to God's Word, we learn how, compared to all of creation, we, as humans, have been made in the image of God (Genesis 1:26). Who we are is a reflection of the God who created us. Therefore, why would we want to become a different image when we have already been created in God's image? When comparison creeps in, remember that you are wondrously made in the image of your Creator. May you embrace how you have been designed and praise the One who formed you.

Action Step

Write Psalm 139:14 on a sticky note, and place it on your mirror to reflect on each day.

Lie:

People think I am _____

When you read the title of this lie, how do you finish the sentence? Maybe you feel as if people think you are unattractive or unintelligent. Maybe you think people view you as too much, too loud, or too quiet. Often, this thought enters our minds when we interact with others or when a certain circumstance involving others occurs. For example, if we stumble over our words in a class presentation, we may worry that our classmates are zeroing in on our weaknesses. Or, when we walk into the cafeteria or a social gathering, we may worry that people are focusing on our flaws or insecurities.

Focusing on others' perceptions is rooted in our fear of man. When we fear man, we allow how others view us to define and influence us. The truth is, what we think others believe about us is most often not even true at all. We are the ones assuming the negative perceptions of others.

But what about when someone else finishes the lie in the title? What if they say that we are unintelligent, unattractive, or too much? This, too, involves the fear of man. When we fear man, the words and opinions of others hold more weight than what God's Word declares about us.

While there are times when we should listen to the words of others, especially if they involve a sin issue in our lives, we were not created to place our identity in the perceptions of others. God created us to worship and glorify Him, but we elevate man over God when we focus more on what others think or say than what God says. In essence, we worship the opinions and perceptions of others when we care more about people's responses than giving God glory. Proverbs 29:25 tells us, "The fear of mankind is a snare, but the one who trusts in the Lord is protected." The fear of mankind is a snare because, like an animal stuck in a trap, we cannot be freed from other people's hold over our lives in our own strength.

We fight the fear of man by fearing the Lord most of all. Instead of fixating on the perceptions of others, we are to focus on worshiping God and being faithful to Him. When we fear the Lord, our gaze will be upward at the God of glory instead of down at flawed mankind. Focusing our attention on pleasing the Lord over pleasing man also reminds us of what is true for us in Christ. When we worship God, we are reminded that we are loved by our heavenly Father (John 15:9), that we receive grace for our weaknesses (2 Corinthians 12:9), and that we are fearfully and wonderfully made (Psalm 139:14).

In addition to worshiping the Lord, we must remain rooted in the truth of God's Word. Scripture should frame and determine our identity, not the thoughts and opinions of others. Worshiping the Lord and resting in the truth of Scripture keeps our identity in Christ alone. When our identity is in Christ, we will not allow the thoughts or opinions of others to sway us. Instead, we will remain secure in who we are in Christ and who God's Word declares us to be.

Action Step

List out three truths declaring who you are in Christ that you can recall and rest in when this lie enters your mind.
Tip: For help getting started, refer to a few of the verses referenced above, including Proverbs 29:5, John 15:9, 2 Corinthians 12:9, and Psalm 139:14.

03

Lie:

I need to do what others want or expect to be affirmed

,,

In Christ, we receive the affirmation we crave.

03

Each one of us longs for affirmation. Saying that we long for affirmation is the same as saying we long for other people's approval. We can look to our friends or a relationship to make us feel good about ourselves, so when we do not feel affirmed, we can end up thinking that we need to do what others want or expect from us. We can believe that once we do these things, others will be pleased with us and we will feel validated. But this mentality can have consequences.

When we think we need to do what others want or expect, we can make sinful choices to please others through sexual sin, drugs, or theft. These choices can harm us or others and create strained or broken relationships. Doing what others want or expect also causes us to act in obedience to other humans. Instead of obedience to God and His Word, we can become consumed with following through with the demands and expectations of others.

Paul writes in Galatians 1:10, "For am I now trying to persuade people, or God? Or am I striving to please people? If I were still trying to please people, I would not be a servant of Christ." Paul's words do not mean that we are no longer servants of Christ when we try to please people, but they do teach us how we can act as servants to man instead of servants of Christ when we aim to please man. We were created to please and obey God, but the sinful nature we have received from the Fall causes us to become enslaved to man. Instead of seeking and receiving our affirmation through our relationship with Christ, our sinful hearts crave and seek affirmation from others.

When we desire affirmation from others, we can end up placing our identity in the reactions of others. Even if we succeed in doing what others want, we may not receive the response we were desiring. Or perhaps we achieve the feeling of validation, only for that person or group of people to reject us. Because our identity has been placed in the responses of others, we can be left hurt, broken, and insecure.

The disappointment and consequences that arise from obeying others' desires and expectations reveal our need for Jesus. In Christ, we receive the affirmation we crave. Instead of the often empty and flawed affirmation of man, our affirmation will come from the truths of the gospel. The gospel reminds us how we are loved, forgiven, chosen, and redeemed in Christ. The truths of the gospel are what give us true affirmation. When we rest in these gospel truths, we will not be as quick to crave and cling to the affirmation of man.

Our relationship with Christ not only gives us true affirmation but also heart transformation. Christ's grace reorients our hearts back to proper worship of God. When we worship God, we will make decisions to obey and please the Lord. We will walk in His wisdom and righteousness. And, through the help of the Spirit, we receive discernment that helps us recognize and stand firm against sinful or foolish requests, as well as the ability to navigate our relationships with others wisely. When we rest in our relationship with Christ, we will enjoy friendships without relying on people to give us only what God can give.

CHRIST'S GRACE REORIENTS OUR HEARTS
BACK TO PROPER WORSHIP OF GOD.

Action Step

Spend some time in prayer confessing to God the ways you seek the affirmation of man, and ask for His help to fear and obey Him.

04

Lie:

I am a failure

The beautiful reality of God's grace is that it never runs dry.

There are moments in each of our lives when we will fail. Maybe you receive a grade for a test you thought you did well on, only to see it is marked with an "F." Or perhaps you miss the winning shot, and your team loses an important game. Whatever it may be, failing at something can be extremely discouraging. If we are not careful, we can allow our failures to cause us to believe that we, ourselves, are failures. Dwelling on the lie that we are failures can cause us to want to give up on our education, hobbies, or future opportunities. While moments of failure are difficult, moments of failure do not have to be debilitating. How, then, can we remain secure even in moments of failure? By resting in Christ's grace.

Jesus gives us His grace for our every failure. Our God knows that we are imperfect people and will make mistakes. Even still, His love for us remains steady, and His grace overflows to us no matter how many times we fail. If we doubt this truth, all we have to do is look to the story of Scripture.

Throughout the Bible, we receive example after example of people who failed. God's chosen people, the Israelites, constantly failed in their obedience and faithfulness to God. The leaders and kings God chose, such as Moses and David, failed in their leadership and personal integrity. But God never gave up on His people, even though they failed Him over and over again.

God's steadfastness to remain committed to His people is displayed most brilliantly at the cross. Through the sacrifice of Christ, God demonstrated His great love for us (Romans 5:8). When we come to know Jesus, we receive God's forgiveness that covers all of our sins, shortcomings, and imperfections. The beautiful reality of God's grace is that it never runs dry. Like those in the Bible, we too will fail in our lives and in our relationships with God, but God's grace remains steadfast. Because of Christ, God does not look at us as failures but as redeemed people.

Knowing that God forgives and does not fault us for our failures allows us to feel at peace when we experience mishaps. Not only this, but moments of failure are also opportunities to rest in Christ's strength. In 2 Corinthians 12:9, Paul writes, "But he said to me, 'My grace is sufficient for you, for my power is perfected in weakness.'" When we fail, we can admit our weakness and inability to be perfect and turn to Jesus, who gives us His strength. We do not have the strength in and of ourselves to pick ourselves up when we stumble and fall. But, in Christ, we have a strong and steady hand that lifts us up and helps us keep going. Psalm 37:24 gives us an example of this as it says, "Though he falls, he will not be overwhelmed, because the Lord supports him with his

GOD'S STEADFASTNESS TO REMAIN COMMITTED TO HIS PEOPLE IS DISPLAYED MOST BRILLIANTLY AT THE CROSS.

hand." God gives us His grace for our stumblings and His strength to persevere.

When we fail, we can take a breath and trust that God will help us. We can fight the lie that we are failures with the truth that we are forgiven. Failure is inevitable, but we have a God whose mercies are new every morning. May we not view ourselves as failures but as redeemed children, loved and aided by our heavenly Father.

Action Step

Memorize a Bible verse that you can recall in the moments you feel like a failure. *Tip: If you are unsure which verse to memorize, choose from one of the verses referenced above, including Romans 5:8, 2 Corinthians 12:9, and Psalm 37:24.*

I need a relationship to feel loved and whole

Each human desires to be loved. There is something that stirs inside us when we watch a romantic movie or read a sweet scene between two lovers in a book. This feeling that we experience can intensify when we watch our friends or siblings enter into relationships, but we remain single. The happy and tender relationships we see on television, in books, and in the lives of the people around us can cause us to believe that a relationship is what we ultimately need to be loved. We can believe that without a relationship, there is a part of us that remains incomplete.

Our world idolizes relationships and perpetuates the idea that we need the love of another to feel complete. But the world's perspective on love differs from Scripture's perspective. While God did create us to be in community with others, we were created first and foremost for God. The longing we experience for love is not ultimately found in a person but in the God who created us. This may be hard for us to accept, especially because God is an invisible God. It can be far easier to seek the love of a person over God because we can feel the embrace and touch of another. But the love or affection we may receive from another is a mere fraction of the love God has for us.

God has demonstrated His incredible love toward us through Christ. John 3:16 tells us, "For God loved the world in this way: He gave his one and only Son, so that everyone who believes in him will not perish but have eternal life." When we enter into a relationship with Christ, we receive the love we have longed to receive. Not only this, but it is Christ's grace and forgiveness that make us whole. Christ's grace forgives our sin and heals our broken relationships with God. The emptiness we try to fill through human relationships is only fully filled with Christ's mercy, love, and forgiveness.

The love we receive through Christ is far greater than the love of another. Why? Because God's love is unconditional and eternal. While human love can be fickle, God's love is forever. And, while human relationships can fail or end, our relationships with God never will. Though we will fail to love God as we should, His love remains steadfast. No matter our sin struggles, imperfections, or weaknesses, our relationship with God remains eternal.

While human relationships can be a gift, we should be careful not to treat them as our main source of love and wholeness. When we depend on human relationships to give us the fullness of love we can only receive through Christ, we will be disappointed. But when we rest in the love of Christ, we will find joy and contentment no matter our relationship status. Even if we do receive the gift of a relationship, we can refrain from placing our identity in our relationships as we remember how "we love because he first loved us" (1 John 4:19). No matter what this world tells us, the only relationship we truly need is a relationship with Christ.

Action Step

Spend some time meditating on the love of Christ, and thank God for His great love for you.

WHEN WE REST IN THE LOVE OF CHRIST, WE WILL FIND JOY AND CONTENTMENT.

06

Lie:

I do not need other people

99

True flourishing happens in community,
not in isolation.

06

It can be easy to convince ourselves that we are self-sufficient people. Unfortunately, our world fuels this belief. People often praise independence and a mentality that declares, *You are the one with the power; you are the only one you can count on!* But we can also fall into self-reliance because of what others have done to us. We may have experienced others letting us down or rejecting us, which can cause us to believe we are better off on our own.

While it is painful to experience being let down or hurt by others, we still need others. In fact, God created us to live in community. While all of our needs are ultimately met by God, God created us to benefit from the relationships around us. In Genesis 2:18, God said that it is not good for man to be alone. God then created Eve as a helper and companion for Adam. Even though Adam and Eve were married, their relationship demonstrated the importance of community. True flourishing happens in community, not in isolation.

By His grace, God uses other people to help, encourage, and hold us accountable. He intentionally uses their friendship and words to speak truth into our lives and give us love and companionship. To reject these relationships is to prevent ourselves from being the people God created us to be. Our growth as humans and as God's people is stunted rather than stimulated when we choose to pull ourselves away from others.

The enemy wants us to believe the lie that we do not need others so that he can pull us into isolation. He knows that isolation is a breeding ground for sin. Community naturally allows us to voice our struggles, but isolation keeps our struggles in the dark. With no one speaking into our lives and holding us accountable, sin can grow like a weed that refuses to be killed. We need other people, especially other believers, who can point out sin issues in our lives. In community, we have the opportunity to confess our struggles and sins and have others keep us accountable. While isolation may seem tempting, community is necessary for our spiritual well-being.

In the moments when self-sufficiency feels like the better option, we must remember our need for people. Ecclesiastes 4:12 says, "A cord of three strands is not easily broken." In other words, there is power in numbers. While we are capable of working on our own, there is greater strength and progress when others are involved. Even if we seek to do life on our own, we will find that we need the help of others at some point. We do not possess the strength to do everything in our own power. When our weaknesses and limitations are apparent, our need for others is realized.

God has uniquely created us for others and has gifted us a life-giving community through the body of Christ. Instead of resolving to live a life apart from others, let us receive the gift of relationships with joy. Even though relationships with others can be messy, the benefits of community make relationships worthwhile. The world and the enemy may tempt us into independence and isolation, but God's Word reveals the value of community. You need others.

BY HIS GRACE, GOD USES OTHER PEOPLE TO HELP, ENCOURAGE, AND HOLD US ACCOUNTABLE.

Action Step

Think of three people in your life who have positively impacted you.

Lie:

I do not need God

Similar to the belief that we do not need others is the belief that we do not need God. Often, we can be tempted to believe we do not need God because of our desire for self-sufficiency. We can think that we are fully capable in our own power to make decisions and do what is right. However, we are finite beings. We have weaknesses and limitations that point out our inability to be self-sufficient. The reality of our weaknesses and limitations reveals our need for God. We were not created to operate in our own power but through the power of the Lord.

As humans, we possess not only weaknesses and limitations but also sinful hearts. Jeremiah 17:9 tells us, "The heart is more deceitful than anything else, and incurable — who can understand it?" We may think our hearts and minds can guide us in the right way to go, but because we are sinful, we will lead ourselves astray. No matter how wise we try to be, we will still make mistakes and stumble into sin.

Our limits and sins point out the fact that God did not design us to be self-sustaining humans. God created each one of us to worship and glorify Him, follow Him, and depend on Him. When we decide that we are the main source of authority in our lives and not God, we sink deeper into sin.

We were not created to operate in our own power but through the power of the Lord.

07

Jeremiah 17:9 reminds us of how deeply sinful our hearts are. Our sin and disobedience deserve punishment because we have sinned against a holy and righteous God. However, there is nothing we can do in our own power to save ourselves from this punishment. Even if we try to be "good" people, our moral choices and good deeds do nothing to release us from the punishment we deserve. Romans 3:11 and 3:23 tell us how there is no one who is righteous and how we all sin and fall short of the glory of God. But this is why we need God. Only God has the power to save us from our sin.

In His kindness, God sent us Jesus to bring us salvation. Through His death and resurrection, Christ gives us grace that covers and cleanses our sinful and prideful hearts. When we come to faith in Christ, we receive His strength and power that help us walk in obedience to God. God's ways lead us to true freedom, not our ways. When we depend on God, submit to His ways, and choose to follow Him, we will make choices that honor and glorify Him. We will live as the holy people He created us to be and experience the freedom of serving Him.

GOD'S WAYS LEAD US TO TRUE FREEDOM, NOT OUR WAYS.

Our fickle hearts may tell us that we do not need God, but we are lost without God. Instead of ignoring our weaknesses, limitations, and sins, let us recognize our utter dependence on the Lord. As we daily admit our need for God and place our dependence on Him, we will rest in His strength, wisdom, and righteousness that help us truly live.

Action Step

List out several ways you need to rely on
God in your life.

_____

_____

_____

_____

_____

_____

_____

_____

_____

08

Lie:
No one understands me

"They just don't understand me." Maybe you have found yourself saying these words after an argument with your parents or a frustrating conversation with a friend. Sometimes we can say this statement with a roll of our eyes, simply shrugging off the temporary annoyance. But other times, these words can linger, and dwelling on them long enough can cause us to feel seriously misunderstood. The more we dwell on these words, the greater chance we have of becoming critical of ourselves or others.

It is hard when we feel misunderstood. We all want to feel known and accepted by others, and being understood plays a part in those desires. When someone does not understand what we are saying, or when someone responds with confusion or negativity over something we do, say, or wear, we can feel awkward, alienated, or perhaps even foolish. On the other hand, it is also possible to use the feeling of being misunderstood as an excuse to sin. We may justify doing something wrong because another person does not "get us." In this way, we can view others' responses to us as their issue—not an issue that reflects upon us. Instead of trying to learn how we can help others understand us better or evaluating whether what we are doing is indeed wrong, we continue with our behavior, no matter the reactions we receive.

However, feeling misunderstood does not have to pull us into either extreme. It is possible to respond to the belief that no one understands us without plunging into despair or excusing sin. How? By the reminder that God completely understands us.

In Psalm 139, David expresses his awe over God's all-knowing nature. He writes, "Lord, you have searched me and known me.

You know when I sit down and when I stand up; you understand my thoughts from far away" (Psalm 139:1–2). God understands us completely because He is omniscient, which means that He is all-knowing. He knows every part of us, even the parts of us we wish we could hide. God understands us completely because He is the One who created us (Psalm 139:3–16). He knows the wiring of our brains, the condition of our hearts, and the unique qualities that make us who we are.

One of the most beautiful truths is that God knows and understands us completely, yet He still chooses to love us. He loves us despite our weaknesses and sins, and He demonstrated His great, unconditional love for us by sending us Jesus. And, because Jesus took on flesh, Jesus too understands us completely. He knows what it is like to be rejected, alienated, and misunderstood. When we feel like no one understands us, we can picture Jesus whispering to us, "I do."

Whenever feelings of shame or sadness arise from feeling misunderstood, we can rest in God's love for us. Through God's strength and wisdom, we can learn how to bring greater clarity to others and help them better understand us. With the help of the Spirit, we can be aware of sinful habits in our lives that we need to repent and turn away from. People will fail to understand us, but we do not have to respond in despair or rebellion. Even if others make us feel misunderstood, we can have peace, knowing that we are completely known and understood by God.

Action Step

Consider talking with a parent, trusted friend, or counselor, and share with them how you are feeling misunderstood.

09

Lie:

I am alone

"

Because of Christ's grace, we are bound together
in a union with God that can never break.

You have nobody. No one cares about you. You are alone. These thoughts can often enter our minds when someone rejects, alienates, or abandons us. Maybe somebody you care about has turned their back on you, no one sits with you in the cafeteria, or your parents spend more time away from you than they do with you. Or perhaps you think these thoughts because you know your friends are hanging out with others while you are home by yourself on a Friday night. Whatever the situation may be, believing that we are alone can cause us to feel as if no one truly loves or cares for us, and we can begin to worry that the people in our lives will eventually leave us. Feeling lonely can also cause us to turn inward and wonder what is wrong with us that we are stuck feeling so alone.

Combating loneliness can be a struggle. Even if you are in a crowded room, you can still feel as if you are all alone. Often, we feel alone because we are not receiving the companionship we desire or the relationship we crave. We may think that if we only had more friends or a boyfriend, we would not feel so alone. However, our feelings of loneliness are not meant to be resolved ultimately through others but through our relationship with God.

God created us for Himself, but sin separates us from Him. Yet God made a way for us to be reunited with Him once again by sending us Jesus. When we come to faith in Christ, we are reconciled, or made right, in our relationship with God once again. Because of Christ's grace, we are bound together in a union with God that can never break. He is ours, and we are His forever. If we are in Christ, we are never alone. We have the presence of God with us always, no matter where we go or what we do. Unlike our human relationships, we can have complete assurance that God will never leave us. As Jesus says in Matthew 28:20, "I am with you always, to the end of the age."

Because God is an invisible God, we may still feel as if we need the physical presence of others to make us feel less alone. However, in these moments of loneliness, God provides us with ways we can become more aware of His presence, even if we cannot physically feel Him. We can experience God's presence when we pray or open up His Word. We can also experience God's presence when we gather with other brothers and sisters in Christ. In fact, one of the ways we can combat loneliness is by remembering that we belong to an eternal family.

The Christian life is not an isolated life, for we are part of the family of God. One day, we will experience what it is like to live with this family forever, but we receive a foretaste of that reality in the present. When we go to church or fellowship with other believers, we are reminded how we are not alone. In His kindness, God uses the physical presence of other believers to remind us of His loving presence with us. But, even on the days when we are apart from others, we are never alone because God is with us.

THE CHRISTIAN LIFE IS NOT AN ISOLATED LIFE, FOR WE ARE PART OF THE FAMILY OF GOD.

Action Step

Think of a couple of people God has placed in your life, and thank God for these people.

10

Lie:
I am insignificant

Each one of us has worth and significance because we are created and loved by God.

You are walking through the hallway at school and find yourself thinking, *Does anyone notice me?* You gaze at everyone around you. The girl with her boyfriend's arm around her shoulders. The guy surrounded by his laughing friends. The group of girls huddled around their lockers. You feel like you are lost within the crowd—maybe even invisible.

It can be easy at times to feel small. Everyone else may seem more important, more popular, or more special. We can look at ourselves in comparison and feel unimportant or worthless. However, to believe we are insignificant is to believe a lie. Each one of us has worth and significance because we are created and loved by God.

Genesis 1:26–27 tells us that we were created in God's image. To be created in God's image is to reflect who God is. A mother may look at her son and say, "You are the spitting image of your father!" In other words, she sees the father's qualities present in her son. In the same way, we reflect God's qualities because we were made in His image. Being created in God's image is a testimony to our significance. When God created the world, He created everything, but only humans were created in His image. This means we have been set apart since the beginning of

10

creation. And we have been set apart to reflect the holy, majestic, and powerful God of all creation.

To be created at all is a testimony to our significance. In God's divine sovereignty and grace, God chose for us to be born and has given each one of us a purpose. But our significance is also revealed through the sacrifice of Christ. Even though we are made in God's image, sin mars God's image in us. Because of sin, we do not naturally reflect the qualities of God but choose to pursue sinful desires and actions. But, although we are sinful and do not deserve salvation, Jesus died on the cross for us. The fact that Jesus went to the cross in our place reveals how much Christ treasures us. We are not worthy of Christ's salvation because of our sin, but Jesus counted the cost of the cross worthwhile because of His great love for us.

We are deemed worthy because of Christ's grace and mercy—not because of anything we have done but because of what Christ has done for us. First Peter 2:9 reminds us of our worth as God's people by saying, "But you are a chosen race, a royal priesthood, a holy nation, a people for his possession, so that you may proclaim the praises of the one who called you out of darkness into his marvelous light." When we feel invisible in a crowded room, we can remember that we are set apart because of Christ. And as God's set-apart people, we get to boast not about ourselves but about the God who saved us.

WE ARE DEEMED WORTHY BECAUSE OF CHRIST'S GRACE AND MERCY—NOT BECAUSE OF ANYTHING WE HAVE DONE

Although our world may assign significance based on appearance or skill, our significance is found in the God who created us and the new life God gave us through His Son. Even if the world makes us feel insignificant, we can remember that we are deeply loved by the God who created us and our Savior who died for us.

Action Step

List three ways God has gifted you.

-
-
-

I will never amount to anything

Going to school during your teenage years can be a time of learning, fun, and development. But school can also feel daunting the closer you get to graduation and adulthood. In the last years of school, there is typically one thing on everyone's mind: *What do I do next?* Of course, some students might have known what they want to do for years, and some might live in an area or culture that mandates their next steps. But, for others of us, figuring out this next step can feel like a mystery.

We can look at our future with uncertainty but also discouragement. For example, we may examine everyone else around us—people who seem smart and like they are "going places"—but then look at our skills or grades and believe we will never amount to anything. Feeling unaccomplished can make us want to give up and even think, *Why pursue anything if we will never amount to anything?* While failure and insecurity can make us feel as if we will never amount to anything, God has a plan for each and every one of us.

In Jeremiah 29:11, God says, "'For I know the plans I have for you'—this is the Lord's declaration—'plans for your well-being, not for disaster, to give you a future and a hope.'" In this context, God was speaking to the people of Israel who had disobeyed Him. While the Israelites had to experience the consequences of exile for their sin, God promised them a future of restoration to give them hope. Just as God knew the plans He had for Israel, so does He know the plans He has for us. However, we can choose not to pursue God's plans. We can take our lives into our own hands and decide how we want to live. But when we walk in obedience to the Lord, we will walk in the plans He has for us. Even if we do not understand God's plans or know all the details, we can trust Him. When we walk in God's plans, we will accomplish His good purposes in our lives.

We can also remember that if we are in Christ, we are being used and shaped by God, for God uses followers of Christ to spread the gospel and build His kingdom on earth. Even if we struggle to know the next step in our lives, we can be confident that whatever God leads us to, He will use us as a gospel witness. But God doesn't just work through us—He also works within us. Philippians 1:6 tells us, "I am sure of this, that he who started a good work in you will carry it on to completion until the day of Christ Jesus."

Although we may doubt our skills and future successes, we can find peace in remembering that we are being sanctified, or becoming more like Christ. The God who started His good work of sanctification in our lives will see this work through to completion. If we are in Christ, we are being sanctified by God and will one day be glorified, or made perfect, by God. Until that day, we can walk in God's plans, knowing that He uses us for His glory and good purposes.

Action Step

Set at least one future goal you can work toward with the help of the Lord.

12

Lie:

I am a burden to others

"

We are not a burden to others because God uses others to help carry our burdens.

12

The lie that we are a burden to others can often enter our minds because of the needs we have. Maybe we feel guilty about the amount of money our parents or guardians pay for our education or extracurricular involvement. Maybe we are struggling with a mental disorder or physical injury and have to rely on someone else's care. Whatever we feel the burden may be, this lie can leave us discouraged and even depressed if we dwell on it long enough.

The lie that we are a burden to others is a lie the enemy loves to perpetuate. The enemy can use this lie to cause us to become bitter with God about our needs, weaknesses, and sufferings. However, instead of succumbing to this lie, we can rest in this important truth from Scripture: We are not a burden to others because God uses others to help carry our burdens.

Galatians 6:2 says, "Carry one another's burdens; in this way you will fulfill the law of Christ." This is not a simple encouragement but a command. As followers of Christ, we are commanded to carry the burdens of others willingly and joyfully. This command reveals to us how God has graciously given us other people to come alongside us and help us. While God supplies His help, strength, and power to us daily, He also works through others who come to our aid. The burdens we experience are not meant to be carried alone. By His grace, God places people in our lives to shoulder the load of our needs, sufferings, and weaknesses.

However, it is possible to bring pain or strain upon others because of foolish or sinful choices. When we make mistakes and get into trouble, we can cause others grief or disappointment because of what we have done. Our decisions carry weight, and our relationships can be affected by the poor and sinful choices we make. Because of this, we should think critically about our decisions and how they might affect our relationships with others. We will all continue to make sinful mistakes throughout our lives. But, in the moments we fail to do what is right, we can rest in Christ's grace.

By His grace, God gives us the gift of other people in our moments and seasons of need. Instead of viewing ourselves as a burden because of our needs, we can be reminded of how others show their love for us as they take care of us. This love is a mere fraction of the love God has for us. God, in His infinite love, sent us Jesus, who willingly carried the burden of our sin and shame on the cross and allowed this burden to crush Him in death. But, three days later, Jesus rose from the dead, declaring His victory not only over the burden of sin—but every burden sin creates.

Just because you carry burdens does not mean you are a burden to others. Our burdens themselves may cause strain as others help carry them, but it is the burdens themselves that are weighty, not the person who is experiencing them. May God's Word remind you that you are not a burden for having limitations and needing the help of others. Even if your burdens are heavy, you are gifted both the strength of others and the strength of God to lift your every weight.

THE BURDENS WE EXPERIENCE ARE NOT
MEANT TO BE CARRIED ALONE.

Action Step

Consider a couple of ways that others are currently showing love to you through their actions.

13

What I do now does not affect the future

We choose to ignore the project due Friday and watch television instead, thinking, *I will get to it eventually*. Our friends persuade us to break curfew, and we say to ourselves, *What is the harm in spending twenty more minutes out?* Our longtime crush finally asks us out, but we choose to ignore the fact that he is not a Christian.

These instances may seem harmless on the surface, but they can lead to consequences. Choosing to put off homework can develop a procrastination habit that can lead to bad grades and issues with getting into college or landing a job. Deciding to break curfew leads us to ignore obedience to our parents and hurt our relationship with them. Dating someone who is a nonbeliever can put us into situations that cause us to compromise our faith.

We may think that what we do does not affect the future, but our actions carry weight. Even the smallest, seemingly insignificant decision can have long-term consequences. When we believe the lie that what we do in the present does not affect our future, we set ourselves up for later struggles, issues, and pain.

One of the greatest biblical examples of this reality is the Fall. Adam and Eve had every-

13

thing they needed when they were in the garden. They had the presence of God, a creation of abundance, and a life of peace and joy. But one single choice would change everything. When Adam and Eve took the fruit from the forbidden tree, they brought sin into the world. Because of their decision, each one of us now has a sinful nature and deserves punishment for our sin.

Jesus says in John 8:34 that "everyone who commits sin is a slave of sin." As slaves to sin, we can form and perpetuate sinful habits in our lives instead of God-honoring habits. These habits can cause us to make light of our decisions and the potential outcome of our actions. But our choices have future and even eternal consequences. This truth should not make us afraid to make decisions, but it should cause us to think seriously about our choices. Our inclination to put off what is important or ignore sinful decisions is why we need Jesus. Only Jesus can free us from being slaves to sin and make us slaves to righteousness instead.

ONLY JESUS CAN FREE US FROM BEING SLAVES TO SIN AND MAKE US SLAVES TO RIGHTEOUSNESS INSTEAD.

We are not wise or strong enough on our own to always do what is right, but when we come to faith in Jesus, we receive His wisdom and strength. We also receive the Holy Spirit, who convicts us of sin, helps us obey God's Word, and gives us the ability to fight against unwise habits or temptations.

However, because of our sinful nature, we will still end up making decisions that can lead to either short or long-term consequences. If we are in Christ, there is grace for these moments. Even if we make a decision that negatively impacts us in the long run, God forgives us and gives us the grace to navigate the consequences of that decision. We can have peace even in the moments we mess up, knowing that God can work through our mistakes for our good and His glory.

Action Step

Take a moment to consider your habits. What are one or two habits you can change that will benefit you in the long run?

14

lie: *Things will never get better*

Have you ever been in a season or situation that felt like it would last forever? Perhaps you are in that place right now. These circumstances can be extremely discouraging. Sometimes it can feel as if God has brought you to this place to leave you there. When a certain circumstance does not change, we can easily believe the lie that our situation will never get better.

The way God works in our lives can seem frustrating. We do not always understand His plans or why He has allowed certain situations or sufferings into our lives. Even still, in His divine sovereignty, God controls the circumstances of our lives for our good and His glory (Romans 8:28). We may not know why God has brought us into certain situations, but we do know that He works through every situation and season — no matter how long they persist. Because of this truth, we can confidently know that things will get better.

However, when and how our circumstances will change depends on God's sovereign will. He may cause a certain situation to persist more than others for a particular reason only He knows. In these moments, we can remember how God works through each and every circumstance, even the hard and the painful, to shape us into the image of Christ. We may not know the "why" behind the situation God has brought us to, but we do know that God is using each situation to transform us into Christlikeness. Therefore, even if our circumstances feel slow to change or change does not happen on this side of eternity, we can lean into such times and be open-handed to how God is sanctifying us in that season.

We can also have hope in hard circumstances by remembering that God is a God of change. From the very beginning of Scripture, we learn how God ordered creation by the words of His mouth. He changed the earth from a place of darkness to a place of life and abundance. And even when humans disobeyed God and brought sin into the world, He continued to work in the lives of His people to bring about change. He promised a covenant of restoration, delivered the Israelites from slavery, and even brought His people back from exile. Many of these people had to wait and trust the Lord as He orchestrated His plan of renewal and restoration, but God was faithful to accomplish His purposes in their lives. Ultimately, God displayed how He is in the business of change and renewal by sending Jesus. Through the death and resurrection of Jesus, those who come to faith in Him have their sins forgiven, their hearts redeemed, and their lives remade.

But God did not cease His work of change after Jesus came. Right here and now, God is orchestrating change through the power of the Spirit as He builds His kingdom on earth. And one day, God will complete His work of change once and for all when He transforms all of creation back into a place of perfect peace. If God has promised to redeem the whole world when He returns, we can have confidence that He will redeem our circumstances. Even if our situations and sufferings persist, we can rest in the truth that God will make all things new.

Action Step

Journal about how you can trust God to work in your circumstances or current season. If you would like, use the space provided on the next two pages.

---

journal —

*I can trust God to work in my
circumstances or current season.*

_____

_____

_____

_____

_____

_____

_____

_____

_____

_____

_____

_____

_____

_____

_____

_____

_____

_____

_____

_____

_____

_____

_____

15

Lie:

I do not fit in

,,

Our desire for acceptance is not meant
to be met in others but in God.

15

Walking into the school cafeteria or canteen can remind us of the different cliques that form in school. Each table likely resembles a group of people who think, dress, and act similarly. Instead of mingling with other groups, these groups often stick together and separate from others who are not like them. As we scan the room with a tray of food in our hands, we may observe these groups from afar, uncertain where we fit into the crowd.

The reactions of others can also make us feel like we do not fit in. Maybe we have experienced people teasing us for how we look or the hobbies we enjoy. Perhaps other students have purposely alienated us in school events or personal get-togethers. Feeling like we do not fit in can often lead us to two responses. The first response is isolation. If we feel like we do not fit in, we can allow ourselves to pull away from people and resolve to be alone. The second response is conformity. We may decide that in order to fit in, we need to think, dress, and act like those we want acceptance from. We can end up changing ourselves in hopes that by doing so, we can finally fit in.

The desire we feel to fit in is connected to our desire for acceptance. It is a natural human desire to want to be accepted and part of a group, so when we are not, we can end up feeling like there is something wrong with us. However, our desire for acceptance is not meant to be met in others but in God. God created us to belong to Him and worship Him. When sin entered the world, sin broke God's perfect relationship with mankind and distorted our worship. Now, we often turn to other people to receive the love and acceptance that is only truly found in God alone. This is why we need Jesus. Jesus is the One who forgives us of our sin and restores our broken relationship with God. Because of Christ, we are fully accepted by God.

Unlike human acceptance, being accepted in Christ is a gift that we do not need to earn or fight to receive. If God fully accepts us, we do not have to search for human acceptance—for we already have all the acceptance we need. Instead of conforming to the standards of others to make us feel accepted, we must rest in the love and acceptance of Christ, for when we do, we will no longer desire validation from others. Our relationships with the people around us will be something to enjoy but not something we need in order to feel whole. Resting in and responding to our relationship with Christ also gives us security when we feel rejected. In the moments when we feel shut out or overlooked, we can rest in the truth that God loves us. Even if others reject us, we can be confident that God never will.

Acceptance in Christ is far greater than the acceptance of man because God's acceptance is eternal. Therefore, let us not look to others to make us feel validated or whole. Our longings for acceptance are satisfied as we remember that we are fully accepted in Christ.

Action Step

Think of a couple of practical ways you can help others feel included this week, and set a goal to accomplish these ways.

HOW I CAN HELP:

GOAL:

16

Lie:

I am unworthy to be loved

Though we were unworthy to receive God's love, because of Christ, we are deemed worthy.

We may desire to experience or feel the love of others but believe we are unlovable. Often, our past or present circumstances influence this belief. For example, past or current sexual sin, a situation of abuse*, or viewing pornography can make us feel ashamed and unlovable. Or perhaps how we have treated our parents or guardians makes us feel unworthy of their love. We can also feel we are unworthy to be loved because of how others treat us. Maybe a parent did or does not treat us with the love we should have received, or a boyfriend or girlfriend hurt us and made us feel unlovable.

We can also feel unworthy to be loved by God. We may read of God's great love and think that other people deserve God's love, but not us. The things we do or have done may seem too shameful for God to love us. The truth is, none of us deserve God's love. Each one of us is a sinner and can do nothing to earn God's love. Yet, even though we do not deserve God's love, God loves us still. We see God's love throughout Scripture in His plan to redeem and save His people. We see His love in His choice to forgive and rescue His people, even though they disobeyed Him. And we see God's love beautifully displayed in Christ. Romans 5:8 says, "But God proves his own love for us in that while we were still sinners, Christ died for us." Though we were unworthy to receive God's love, because of Christ, we are deemed worthy.

If we still doubt this to be true, we must remember the power of God's love. God's love is unconditional, which means that His love is not based on what we have done, are doing, or will do. It is not influenced by our looks, skills, or successes. God's love is not determined by our actions or mistakes but by His abundant love and mercy. This gives us supreme comfort that there is nothing we can do that will prevent God from loving us. And, if we are in Christ, we can be confident that there is nothing we can do to remove God's love from us. Romans 8:38–39 says that nothing can separate us from the love of God. Not our past. Not our mistakes. Not our struggles. Nothing. The love of God that we receive through Christ is ours forever.

> GOD'S LOVE IS NOT DETERMINED BY OUR ACTIONS OR MISTAKES BUT BY HIS ABUNDANT LOVE AND MERCY.

But then, how does the love of God impact the unworthiness we feel to be loved by others? Though there are people who can treat us as unworthy and unlovable, there are also people who will love us despite our problems and mistakes. When others love us in this way, it is a reflection of the gospel. Our ability to forgive and love others despite their sins displays the beauty of the gospel and the love and forgiveness of God. Yet it is not the love of humans that determines our worth. It is Christ who has made us worthy, and it is in Christ that we find our worth. When feelings of unworthiness arise, we can rest in the love of Christ and remember our worth in Him.

Action Step

Memorize Romans 8:38–39. For tips on how to memorize Scripture, refer to page 8.

*If you have experienced abuse, please communicate this to a trusted adult. God grieves over this pain, and it is not something you have to endure on your own.

17

Lie:

God does not love me

While we can believe that we are unworthy to be loved by God, we may also believe that God does not love us. Perhaps the same reasons behind the previous lie apply to this lie, as well. But maybe there are other reasons we believe this lie to be true. Maybe we struggle to read our Bibles or pray consistently, so we assume God is upset with us because of these struggles. Or maybe we fail in being obedient to God's Word by saying things we know we shouldn't or by disobeying our parents, so we think God has removed His love from us because of our sin. These struggles, sins, and failures can lead us to believe the lie that God does not love us.

As we learned previously, God's love is unconditional. This is good news for the days or seasons we feel as if God's love has run dry. Even if we mess up in our faithfulness to God or fail to obey God's Word, if we are in Christ, we can be confident that God does and always will love us. In the moments we struggle to believe that God loves us, we should remember and reflect on the gospel. Gazing at the gospel reminds us of Christ's insurmountable love for us. First John 3:16 tells us, "This is how we have come to know love: He laid down his life for us." Each of us is a sinner who pursues our own desires rather than obeying God. But Christ has demonstrated His love for us through His sacrifice on the cross, and when we trust and believe in Jesus, we receive grace and forgiveness for our sin.

The fact that God sent us Jesus even though we were dead in our sins speaks to His great love for us. And, because of God's unconditional love, we do not have to believe the lie that God's love is for others but not for us. All of us are guilty, and no one possesses a quality that makes them worthy or favorable in the eyes of God. It is only through Christ that we are deemed worthy and favorable. Therefore, because God loves the whole world, and His love is unconditional, we can be certain that He loves us, too. And we experience His great love when we come to know Jesus.

When we trust in Jesus and repent from our sin, God's love is poured into our hearts through the Holy Spirit (Romans 5:5). As believers, we continue to experience the love of God daily. The love of God becomes deeper and sweeter the more we walk with the Lord and grow in our understanding of Him. And if we are in Christ, we have security each day that God's love remains. Lamentations 3:22–23 tells us how God's mercies are new every morning. The mercy we receive through Jesus is a mercy that remains for the rest of our days. Because of God's grace and faithfulness, He gives us His love and mercy every day. This means that even when we fail in our faithfulness or obedience, God's love remains, and His mercy is ours, just as it was the day before.

Action Step

Write down three truths from God's Word that you can recall when you feel as if God does not love you. For example, using 1 John 3:16, you might write, "God loves me so much that He died for me." *Tip: If you're not sure where to start, consider turning to a few of the following verses: John 3:16, 1 John 4:7–8, 1 John 4:9–11, 1 John 4:16, Romans 8:37–39.*

18

Lie:

My sexuality is determined by how I feel or what culture tells me

"

God is love, and true love is not experienced until it aligns with His law and design.

18

Living in today's western culture can be rather confusing. We have celebrities who have changed genders, television shows promoting same-sex relationships, and books about living our own truth. Many of us know and are friends with people who have embraced a new sexual identity or promoted an ideology that says you can be whatever gender you want to be or even that gender is a social construct. Maybe you have even wrestled with your own gender or sexual identity and only feel more confused and unsure what to think. And, if you are struggling with same-sex attraction or feel as if you were born in the wrong body, what our world teaches can seem appealing and possibly even true.

But God's Word tells us something different than our culture's message. Scripture tells us how our sexuality is not determined by how we feel or what culture tells us but by God's good design and law. Society may say that gender can be fluid, but God's Word tells us that gender is fixed. Genesis 1:27 says, "So God created man in his own image; he created him in the image of God; he created them male and female." Gender is a beautiful design from God. Each one of us is created male or female purposefully by God, and we are meant to glorify God with the gender in which we were created. To try and change our sexuality is to oppose and alter who God created us to be.

Scripture also tells us God's design for marriage. Genesis 2:24 says, "This is why a man leaves his father and mother and bonds with his wife, and they become one flesh." This verse describes the intentional union husbands and wives share in marriage. God designed marriage and dating relationships to be between one man and one woman. While some may view this as denying humans the right to love whomever they please, it is God who has determined what love is and the boundaries for that love to be expressed and experienced.

God's Word makes it clear that we are not to step outside of God's design for marriage and sexuality (Hebrews 13:4, Romans 1:26–27). Doing so is a sin and disobeys God's law. Our culture may proclaim the mantra that "love is love," but God is love, and true love is not experienced until it aligns with His law and design. This truth can be hard to grasp, not only because of some cultures' teachings but also because of our personal feelings. The attraction we may feel toward someone of the same sex might feel right to us, but these feelings go against God's law and definition of love. And we might think that changing our bodies will make us our truest selves, but our truest selves are lived out by God's design, not our own.

There is good news for those of us who struggle with same-sex attraction or experience the desire to change our sexuality. In Christ, we are given the strength to deny ourselves and obey God. This may be hard, but we have God's help through the power of the Spirit. In obedience to the Lord, we find freedom and the ability not to live our truth but God's truth. Our world may not view obedience to God as freedom, but living as God created us to be makes us truly free.

OUR TRUEST SELVES ARE LIVED OUT BY GOD'S DESIGN, NOT OUR OWN.

Action Step

Consider how you would respond to someone who asked you your opinion about sexuality. How would you use God's Word to answer them with truth and love?

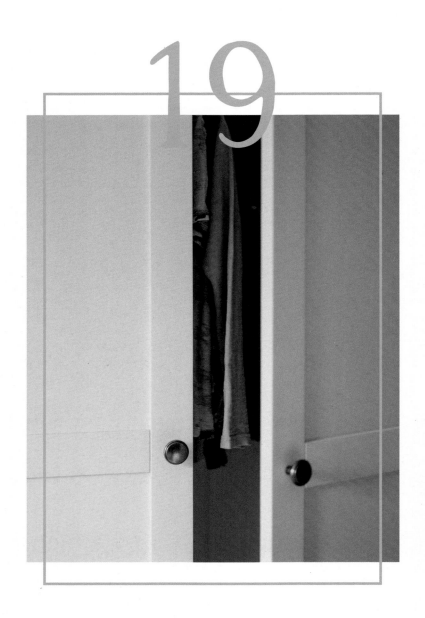

19

There is something wrong with me

We may be broken, but in God's eyes, we are beloved.

Each one of us has different skills, features, and abilities. These differences are meant to be celebrated, but we can criticize them instead. Often, we zero in on our differences when we compare ourselves to others. If the people we compare ourselves to happen to be more popular or skilled than us, we can look at ourselves and assume we are flawed. We may also believe that we are flawed if others tease us. Maybe someone has made fun of a hobby we enjoy, a personal quirk we possess, or the type of clothing we wear. Or perhaps we have a certain physical, medical, or sensory diagnosis that hinders our movements, learning, or capabilities, and we receive stares or whispered comments. These looks and words can sink in deep and penetrate our hearts, causing us to believe that there must be something wrong with us.

In a sense, there is something wrong with each one of us. God created us in His image, and before the Fall, humans were perfect. But sin replaced perfection with imperfection. Now, every person is flawed and broken because we are no longer the holy people God created us to be. When we come to faith in

19

Christ, we are cleansed and made new, but we still have a sinful nature. One day, all those who believe in Jesus will be made fully new and will have no spot or stain ever again. But for now, we live in what is called the already-but-not-yet, which means if we are in Christ, we are made new but still fallen. Because we live on this side of eternity, we will still encounter weaknesses and struggles because of sin.

And, because of sin, we can experience problems and pains we were never meant to experience. Sin creates brokenness, and each one of us experiences brokenness in different ways. However, while the world—and even we—can look down on our types of brokenness, God does not. We might feel shame over the parts of us we cannot control, but God's love and grace assure us that there is no need to be ashamed. We may be broken, but in God's eyes, we are beloved.

But how, then, should we view our differences? We should view them as a gift! No one person is the same, and that is a good thing. Some of us are extroverted, while others are more introverted. Some of us are skilled in sports, and others are better at art or music. Some of us were born with a different skin color, height, and type of hair than others. All of these qualities and abilities make us unique, and they are to be celebrated instead of criticized. While sinful mankind too often criticizes what is meant to be celebrated, we can rejoice over how God made us. We can even celebrate if we have a physical, medical, or sensory diagnosis because God uses our unique situations and capabilities to help others see the world in new and different ways.

OUR BROKENNESS IS MET WITH THE LOVE OF CHRIST.

We all are broken and have differences, but we can view ourselves through His eyes when we turn to Jesus and rest in His grace. Our brokenness is met with the love of Christ.

Action Step

List out three unique qualities about yourself, and thank God for these qualities.

20

I need to follow my heart

"Listen to your heart." "Follow your heart; it knows the right way." We often find this idea in music lyrics, social media quotes, and designs on clothing. On the surface, the encouragement to follow our hearts sounds like good advice. If our minds are overwhelmed, our hearts will show us what to do, right? Unfortunately, this wisdom of the world does not take into consideration the sinfulness of our hearts and the limits of our understanding. Following our hearts leads us astray, but following the Lord leads us on the path of life.

One of the greatest biblical examples of this truth is Solomon. Solomon's story starts strong as Solomon is crowned king over Israel and given wisdom from the Lord. God promises Solomon that if he has a heart of integrity and does what is right, he will have a reign of success and a lasting kingdom. However, Solomon allows himself to marry many foreign women, disobeying God's commands to not intermarry with other nations. First Kings 11:2–3 tells us these sad words, "To these women Solomon was deeply attached in love. He had seven hundred wives who were princesses and three hundred who were concubines, and they turned his heart away." Solomon followed his heart, and his heart led him away from the Lord and into ruin.

Solomon's testimony teaches us the consequences of following our hearts. Because our hearts are desperately sinful (Jeremiah 17:9), our hearts will naturally cause us to be wayward rather than wise. But what should we listen to and follow then? Proverbs 3:5–6 says, "Trust in the Lord with all your heart, and do not rely on your own understanding; in all your ways know him, and he will make your paths straight." Without a relationship with Jesus, we cannot trust the Lord with all our hearts. Our sin blinds us to true wisdom and influences us to rely on our understanding. But, when we come to faith in Christ, Jesus's grace and forgiveness open our eyes and cleanse our hearts. Our old sinful hearts that desired to follow their own ways are replaced with hearts that desire to obey and follow the Lord (Jeremiah 31:33). However, even though we have redeemed hearts, we still have sinful flesh that will seek to follow our own feelings and desires. Yet, when we rest in the power of the Spirit and trust the Lord, we will not be led by our own understanding.

As we seek to rest in the Spirit and trust the Lord, we should also remain rooted in God's Word. God's Word gives us direction, wisdom, and discernment. Hebrews 4:12 tells us, "For the word of God is living and effective and sharper than any double-edged sword, penetrating as far as the separation of soul and spirit, joints and marrow. It is able to judge the thoughts and intentions of the heart." When we struggle to know if the intentions of our hearts are pure, God's Word gives us discernment. And, in the moments we still feel uncertain, we can trust that the Lord will lead us down the right path—His path. We will never be led astray when we follow the Lord rather than our hearts.

Action Step

Think of a time when you followed your heart, and it led to trouble. What would you have done differently knowing the outcome?

21

Lie:
If it feels good,
I should do it

"

We should not settle for short-term gratification
but seek joy and wisdom in Christ.

21

Similar to the lie that we need to follow our hearts is the lie that we should do what feels good. It can be hard for us to see this as a lie because if something feels good, we can assume it must be a good thing. And in some ways, this is true. In His kindness and grace, God created us to experience joy and pleasure. He filled this world with good things for us to delight in and enjoy. But God also created limits and boundaries for pleasures. While Scripture speaks of the pleasures of wine (Psalm 104:15), it also speaks against drunkenness and establishes drunkenness as a sin (Ephesians 5:18). Sex, too, is designed to give God glory and humans pleasure, but it is also designed to be experienced within the confines of marriage (Matthew 19:5). So Scripture teaches us how God intended us to experience pleasure in accordance with His law.

Often, the idea that "if it feels good, I should do it" is focused on satisfying our desires. But God's good gifts and granted pleasures are ultimately for His glory. We are to be God-glorifying, not self-seeking or self-satisfying in our pursuit of pleasure. This mentality is also connected with instant gratification. As humans—and as teens, in particular—we experience emotions and hormones that almost compel us toward what we think will make us happy and feel good. In pursuit of this satisfaction, we can make quick decisions to achieve that gratification without thinking through the potential consequences of those actions. This is why some of us can fall into sexual sin or the temptation to try drugs or alcohol. We can allow the pursuit of pleasure to cloud our judgment, and it may be only after the fact that we realize we have made a mistake and done wrong.

These examples demonstrate how the pursuit of pleasure can result in pain in the short or long term if we operate to receive instant gratification. What are we to do, then? We should not settle for short-term gratification but seek joy and wisdom in Christ. When we seek joy in Christ, we will not depend on temporary pleasures to give us what only Christ can give us. Instead of giving in to pleasures so that we feel satisfied, we can turn to Jesus and rest in the joy that comes from Him.

And when we seek wisdom in Christ, we will receive discernment to understand what pleasures are God-honoring and which ones are not. As we seek the wisdom of the Lord, we will walk in His ways and experience pleasures rightly.

But, because our flesh is weak, we still find ourselves giving into pleasures that are unwise as believers. Thankfully, this is why we have God's Word and the Holy Spirit. Scripture provides us insight into the boundaries God has given us for partaking in certain pleasures. The Holy Spirit provides us with the strength to resist sinful pleasures and helps us navigate pleasures with wisdom. The Holy Spirit also brings us conviction when we partake in unholy pleasures and equips us with self-control to not repeat the same actions. As we remain obedient to God's Word and reliant on the Holy Spirit, we will experience pleasure as God commanded and designed.

AS WE SEEK THE WISDOM OF THE LORD, WE WILL WALK IN HIS WAYS AND EXPERIENCE PLEASURES RIGHTLY.

Action Step

Consider one way you seek pleasure in an unhealthy way. Research practical ways to break any unhealthy habit, and begin to apply at least one of those ways this week.

Lie:

I have to do everything perfectly

We cannot do anything in our own power to make ourselves holy, but that is why God gave us Jesus.

Something we tend to do as humans is pressure ourselves to be perfect, and this makes sense because of the world in which we live. People praise strength more than weakness and often frown upon imperfections. Because of this, we can feel as if we need to do everything perfectly all the time in order to be liked, affirmed, and accepted. If you are a student, perhaps you place pressure upon yourself to get perfect grades. Or, if you play sports, perhaps you place pressure on yourself to always score the goal and never lose. Other people can also place expectations upon us to be perfect. Your parents might be overly critical of you if you get lower than an "A" on a test, or your coach might yell at you for missing an important point. These instances can cause us to crack under pressure and feel ashamed of our failures.

Even though we may experience the pressure or desire to be perfect, only God is perfect. It is God and God alone who has no weaknesses and limitations — He alone possesses the inability to fail. However, we can forget or push off this truth and believe that we can be like God. We can do everything in our power

22

to never fail and make no mistakes. But this is an impossible feat. No one is perfect, and no one can be perfect.

This truth should cause us to relax our shoulders and let out a breath. It should encourage us to stop pursuing unattainable goals and accept who we are—human. However, because we are human, we are sinful. To accept that we are imperfect does not mean we should excuse sin or stop being motivated. We may not be perfect, but we are still held to a standard—God's standard.

God's standard is not perfection but holiness. God created mankind to be holy people who obeyed and glorified Him. But sin tainted what was once holy, and now each one of us fails to achieve God's standard. We cannot do anything in our own power to make ourselves holy, but that is why God gave us Jesus. Our perfect Savior died on the cross in our place so that we could be forgiven. His grace covers our sins and makes us holy and pure. If we are in Christ, we are called to live lives of holiness in response to the forgiveness we have received. Second Timothy 1:9 tells us, "He has saved us and called us with a holy calling, not according to our works, but according to his own purpose and grace, which was given to us in Christ Jesus before time began."

THE PURSUIT OF HOLINESS ALLOWS US TO REMOVE PERFECTION'S PRESSURE AND WALK IN HUMBLE FAITHFULNESS TO THE LORD.

It is a gift that God calls us to holiness rather than perfection. The pursuit of holiness allows us to remove perfection's pressure and walk in humble faithfulness to the Lord. And, because of Christ's grace and the power of the Spirit, we can pursue holiness without feeling overwhelmed. We will fail in our holiness because of our sinful flesh, but Christ gives us His grace. So instead of aiming for perfection, aim for holiness. Seeking perfection burdens us, but walking in holiness gives us freedom.

Action Step

Consider one area of your life in which you feel the need to be perfect. What truths from God's Word can you remember when the impulse for perfection arises in this area? *Tip: If you're not sure where to start when it comes to finding truths from God's Word, consider looking up the following verses: 2 Corinthians 12:9–10, 2 Timothy 1:9, Ephesians 2:8–9, Titus 3:4–5.*

23

Lie: Why feelings and emotions control and define me

You raise your voice at your parents for taking away your phone. You wake up in the morning feeling sad, even though you don't know why. You feel a rush of fear before you give your class presentation. Anger, sadness, and fear are but several of many other emotions and feelings we may experience. For some of us, these feelings and emotions come and go, but for others, they dominate our everyday lives.

When we describe our emotions or feelings, we often say, "I'm angry," or "I'm sad." But, when emotions or feelings regularly occur, we may be tempted to believe that those responses control, own, and define us. This belief can cause our feelings and emotions not just to be something we experience but rather a part of who we are — our identity. Even though emotions and feelings like anger, sadness, and fear are frustrating and discouraging, we do not have to believe the lie that they define us. Who we are in Christ defines us most of all.

It is important to remember that God gifted us with emotions and feelings. Our emotions and feelings are meant to reveal what is in our hearts. Often, but not always, anger can be a sign that we need to work on patience and forgiveness with others. And, even though sadness or fear can point us to a hormonal imbalance, it is possible for these feelings to reveal a misplaced trust in the Lord. When we avoid the hard but necessary task of examining our emotions and feelings and their root cause, it can become easy to succumb to our emotions and feelings. Instead of understanding and evaluating how we can train our emotions, we can make the excuse that how we feel and act is just who we are.

But, when we remember that who we are in Christ defines us, we can look at our emotions and feelings through the lens of the gospel. In doing so, we see how, because of our relationship with Christ, it is Jesus who owns us—not our emotions and feelings. And, because Christ set us free from the power of sin, we also see how our emotions and feelings do not ultimately control us. We might not be able to control when certain emotions and feelings arise, but we can control our response to them. The Holy Spirit helps us fight against sinful responses to our feelings and gives us the strength to react in godly ways to our emotions. And, even if sadness or fear is a lifelong battle, we can remember that this battle will not last forever. When Christ returns, He will deliver us from all that plagues us in the present, and we will live in eternal peace.

Until that day, we can continue with God's help to navigate our emotions and feelings with wisdom. We can rest in His strength when fighting fear is difficult, and we can rest in His peace when sadness arises. And, when the enemy tries to make us believe that our emotions and feelings define us, we can rest in the truth that we are not our anger, fear, or sadness—we are the Lord's.

Action Step

Using the chart on the next page, look up the passage listed with each emotion, and list how you can apply the truth from that verse when you experience that emotion.

Scripture for emotions

Emotion	Scripture	How can I apply the truth of Scripture when I experience this emotion?
Fear	Psalm 56:3–4	
Anger	James 1:19–20	
Jealousy	James 3:14–17	

Joy	Romans 15:13	
Resentment	Ephesians 4:31–32	
Sadness	Psalm 34:17–18	

24

Lie:

I am unforgivable

Our God is a God who is slow to anger, abounds in faithful love, and forgives iniquity and rebellion.

You did it again. The sin that you swore you would never repeat. That bad habit that you have prayed so hard to quit. Shame overwhelms you, and tears fill your eyes. *God cannot possibly forgive me,* you think to yourself.

Our tendency to struggle to obey God as believers can be discouraging. And, if our view of the Lord is skewed, we can believe that God is holding up a chalkboard, waiting to draw strike three and declare us out of His grace. But that is not the God we serve. Our God is a God who is slow to anger, abounds in faithful love, and forgives iniquity and rebellion (Numbers 14:18). To declare these truths further, God sent us Jesus, whose blood covers our iniquity and whose grace deems us forgiven. If we are in Christ, we have full confidence that the forgiveness we receive through Jesus is ours forever. Even on our worst days, God's grace remains.

This means that if we are in Christ, there is nothing we have done or will do that will remove God's grace from us. Because of Christ, God fully and eternally forgives us. As 1 John 1:9 proclaims, "If we confess our sins, he is faithful and righteous to forgive us our sins and to cleanse us from all unrighteousness." This should bring us incredible comfort when we falter in our faithfulness to the Lord. As believers, we have complete assurance that God forgives our every sin—past, present, and future.

But maybe there are still some of us who feel as if what we have done is truly unforgivable. Perhaps we have done something that others would view as the worst possible sin. Throughout the Gospels, we receive example after example of sinful people who encountered the grace of Christ. During Jesus's time on earth, He forgave women caught up in sexual sin (John 8:10–11), dishonest tax collectors (Luke 19:1–10), and His disciples who abandoned Him (John 21:15–19). Even as Jesus hung on the cross, He forgave the thief next to Him and prayed for God's mercy to be upon those who mocked Him (Luke 23:34, 39–43). Christ's forgiveness in the Gospels demonstrates how there is no one too sinful to receive Christ's grace. Jesus invites all sinners to come to

Him and be forgiven. Even what seems unforgivable to us remains forgivable in Christ.

Because Christ's grace was not given to us based on what we have done but because of what Christ has done, we can be confident that Christ's grace remains overflowing forever. The cross of Christ and the blood of Jesus stand as a reminder of Christ's permanent forgiveness. Therefore, in the moments the enemy whispers to us that we are unforgivable, we can look to the cross and listen to the voice of our Savior that calls us forgiven. We can freely confess our sins and continue to seek holiness as we rest in God's forgiveness. Because of Jesus, we are declared innocent in the eyes of God no matter the sin that taints our hearts or plagues our past, for even the dirtiest stains of sin have been washed clean by Jesus's grace.

BECAUSE OF WHAT CHRIST HAS DONE, WE CAN BE CONFIDENT THAT CHRIST'S GRACE REMAINS OVERFLOWING FOREVER.

Action Step

Spend some time in prayer, thanking God for His forgiveness and asking God to help you regularly remember and rest in His grace.

25

Lie:

I need the latest technology and trends to be happy

Our satisfaction is not found in the things of this world. Our satisfaction is found in Christ alone.

If we turn on the television or watch a YouTube video, we see commercials seeking to sell us something. We might see a bunch of people laughing and holding the same drink or someone driving a car and receiving the attention of an attractive person. These commercials are not just trying to sell us a product but a story or message. In viewing those scenes, we may be led to think that we need that drink in order to be popular or have lots of friends, or we need that car to be appealing to the opposite sex.

Commercials and advertisements proclaim the lie that we need a certain product to be happy, but social media can also fuel this lie. We can see images of influencers wearing the latest trends or promoting the newest phone, and we can think we need to have those things to feel happy, satisfied, and affirmed. But the narrative that social media and commercials often seek to tell always fails to fulfill. We may buy those clothes or that new phone, only to find ourselves still dissatisfied and craving the next best thing. This dissatisfaction we and so

25

many others feel is meant to point to the fact that our satisfaction is not found in the things of this world. Our satisfaction is found in Christ alone.

One of the reasons we can so easily forget this truth is because we settle for quick doses of contentment and joy. We make a purchase or receive something we desire, and we experience that instant feeling of gratification. But quick doses of contentment do not provide lasting contentment. We might think we are satisfied, but just as hunger pains come again after a meal, the craving for contentment always returns. While many choose to ignore this reality and keep going to temporary sources for satisfaction, we do not have to operate this way as followers of Christ. As believers, we have all that we need in Jesus. This is why Paul says in Philippians 4:12–13, "In any and all circumstances I have learned the secret of being content—whether well fed or hungry, whether in abundance or in need. I am able to do all things through him who strengthens me."

Even though Paul experienced both seasons of abundance and need, he knew that he could be content in either circumstance because of his relationship with Christ and his contentment in Him. When we place our contentment in Christ, our joy will not rise or fall depending on our circumstances or needs. In Christ, our contentment and joy remain secure. And, because we are placing our contentment in an eternal God, our satisfaction in Christ is long-lasting. We no longer need to

IN CHRIST, WE FIND TRUE JOY AND LASTING SATISFACTION.

settle for temporary morsels when we are feasting on the Bread of Life.

However, our flesh will cause us to still desire the things of this world to feel happy and satisfied. In the moments we find ourselves tempted by temporary pleasures, let us remember the supremacy of Christ. It is our salvation in Christ and our relationship with Him that make us truly satisfied. May we turn away from what the world proclaims is necessary and rest in the One who is our greatest necessity. In Christ, we find true joy and lasting satisfaction.

Action Step

Consider one or two items you are currently clinging to for satisfaction. Come up with one practical way to lessen your hold on this thing or things so that your satisfaction can be rooted in Christ alone.

26

Lie: I can do what I want with my body

The slogan "my body, my choice" is a common mantra in western culture. Over the years, we have seen a rise in people publicly declaring their own bodily autonomy—or the belief that a person should have the right to control what happens with his or her body. While our bodies should certainly be protected from being taken advantage of and exploited, this line of thinking can easily be twisted to support ideas that go against God's good design for our bodies. This can be seen in exercising unhealthy eating habits, entertaining negative thoughts about our bodies, engaging in premarital sex, or perhaps through such measures as having an abortion or undergoing gender transition. If you find yourself in the midst of making decisions like these and are able to change course, Christ offers you His strength to do so. And, if you have already carried out any of these decisions, know that there is grace and hope, and you are washed clean by the blood of Christ when you come to Him in repentance.

Believing that we can do what we want with our bodies denies the One for whom and the reason for which our bodies were created. In pursuing our own rights, we can become self-seeking and self-glorying rather than God-glorifying. Our bodies were created as worship vessels for God. We were designed to glorify God with our bodies by our actions. However, because of sin, we do not naturally use our bodies in glorifying ways. We use our bodies to carry out our sinful desires and disregard the purpose for which our bodies were created. But, when we come to faith in Jesus, our desires and allegiance change. We no longer seek to serve ourselves but the Lord. Our sin nature will complicate these desires, but ultimately as believers, we should seek to give God glory above all else.

The Bible tells us that if we are in Christ, our bodies belong to Him, not us. First Corinthians 6:19–20 says, "Don't you know that your body is a temple of the Holy Spirit who is in you, whom you have from God? You are not your own, for you were bought at a price. So glorify God with your body." These verses teach us how, as believers, our bodies are like temples. Just as the temple was where God's presence dwelt in Bible times, our bodies are now temples because the Holy Spirit dwells within us. And, just as the temple was a place of worship, our bodies are to be used as sacrificial worship to the Lord (Romans 12:1). For our bodies to be worship vessels means our bodies are primarily not for our glory but God's. Not only this, but the blood of Christ has also purchased our bodies. Another way of looking at this is that if you purchase something, that object is yours. In the same way, because we have been purchased by the blood of Christ, we belong to Him. And, since we belong to Him, we are not our own. Therefore, we must use all of who we are — including our bodies — to serve and glorify Him.

This truth impacts every decision we make with our bodies, even down to the clothes we wear. Before we make choices about our bodies, we should ask ourselves, "Is this glorifying God or glorifying me?" or "Am I doing this with my body to please myself or please God?" And, in the moments we are unsure what is the right decision to make about our bodies, we should spend time in prayer or seek the counsel of a parent or mature believer. As we pursue wisdom and seek to worship God with all of who we are, we will make choices with our bodies that honor and glorify the Lord.

Action Step

List three ways you can glorify God with your body this week.

27

Lie:

I am in control of my life

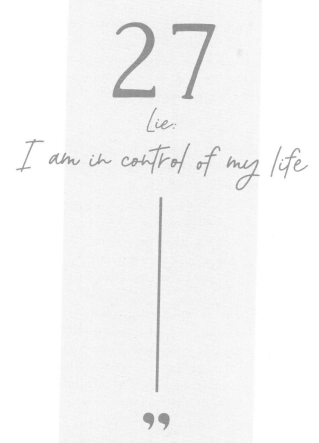

"

While God graciously allows us to make choices,
He is the One who is ultimately in control.

27

William Ernest Henley once wrote, "I am the master of my fate, I am the captain of my soul." This quote and others with the same message promote the idea that humans have individual autonomy—that we are the ones who set the course of our paths and the ones who are ultimately in control of our lives. And, because of sin, we operate this way more often than we might realize. Our sinful flesh desires to be in charge. We like to be the ones who take the steering wheel instead of releasing it into God's hands. This is why it can be a struggle to obey God's commands, even if we are followers of Jesus. We can experience the tension between desiring to do what God says and desiring to do what we want. But, while God graciously allows us to make choices, He is the One who is ultimately in control.

The truth that God is ultimately in control is connected with God's sovereignty. God's sovereignty means that He controls the world and the events that take place within our world. This does not mean that God always causes something to happen, but in His divine sovereignty, He works through everything to accomplish His purposes. However, God also graciously grants humans free will. He allows us to make choices and plans, and because we are given free will, we are the ones who are held responsible for the choices we make and the consequences of those actions. But thankfully, God is the One who works through our decisions and plans. The Lord's purposes will always come to fruition, no matter our choices and actions. As Proverbs 19:21 tells us, "Many plans are in a person's heart, but the Lord's decree will prevail."

The truth that God is the One who is ultimately in control is meant to humble us and motivate us to yield to God's sovereignty. The gift of free will is not a license to do what we please with no thought to the consequences of our actions. It is not permission to ignore God's ultimate authority and sovereignty and seek to be the ones in power. Unfortunately, this is what happened when sin entered the world. It was Adam and Eve's choice to ignore God's commands and resist obedience to His ultimate authority. Thankfully, because God is good and sovereign, He worked through the folly of Adam and Eve to put forth a plan of redemption. He saved us from the error of our ways by sending us Jesus. But, when we come to faith in Christ, we are to submit to Him completely. We are to deny ourselves and take up our cross to follow Jesus (Mark 8:34).

The life of faith is a life of releasing our control to trust in God's ultimate control. It involves laying down our own will so we can submit to God's will. While we can believe that placing control in our own hands leads to true freedom, trusting in God's plans and obeying His ways is what leads to true freedom. Therefore, let us surrender our grip on our lives and submit to the God who holds our lives in His hands.

THE LORD'S PURPOSES WILL ALWAYS COME TO FRUITION, NO MATTER OUR CHOICES AND ACTIONS.

Action Step

Consider one area of your life in which you are currently struggling to give God control. Spend some time in prayer, asking God to help you surrender control to Him and trust Him in this area.

I will never heal from this broken heart

You lie on your bed with tears streaming down your face. Your heart feels broken, and your body is overcome with grief. You ask yourself, *Will I feel like this forever?* It appears like it will last forever in the moment—like your shattered heart will never repair. The pain feels too real and heavy to ever lift.

When we experience heartbreak or grief, whether from a breakup, loss, or rejection, it can certainly seem like we will never heal. But while heartbreak and grief are hard, we do not have to feel as if our wounds will remain. We have a God who comforts us in our pain and has the power to heal our every wound.

Psalm 34:18 tells us, "The Lord is near the brokenhearted; he saves those crushed in spirit." In our moments of grief and despair, God is with us. He is near us in our suffering, and His presence resides with us in our pain. This verse does not only promise God's nearness but also His salvation. Because our God is a God of salvation, we can be confident that God will bring us out of our suffering, even if it takes time. Second Corinthians 1:3–4 says, "Blessed be the God and Father of our Lord Jesus Christ, the Father of mercies and the

If Christ has healed our greatest wound, He can surely heal our lesser wounds.

28

God of all comfort. He comforts us in all our affliction…" God comforts our broken hearts. He is the God of all comfort, which means that His comfort is better than anything this world can supply. And He comforts us in all our affliction. We might believe that our suffering is too great for God's comfort, but God comforts us in all of our afflictions, no matter how great they may seem.

Ultimately, we can be confident that God will heal our wounds because He has done so through Christ. Through the sacrifice of Christ, we receive salvation that heals the wounds of our sin and shame. His grace heals our broken hearts and makes them whole in Him. And, if Christ has healed our greatest wound, He can surely heal our lesser wounds. Yet this healing may take time. Some of us who are experiencing great loss may find that God's healing will be a slow process over an extended amount of time, while others of us might find that this healing takes place faster than we originally thought. However, while we wait for healing, our greatest comfort is the truth that Christ will make all things new. This pain that we are feeling will not last forever because one day, Christ will remove all pain forever. Even if ultimate healing does not occur in this life, we can be confident that it will happen in the next.

GOD COMFORTS OUR BROKEN HEARTS.

But for now, as we experience our grief and pain, we can lean into the arms of the God of comfort. We can rest in His peace and strength that helps us move forward, even in our brokenness. We can even rejoice, knowing that God will bring us out of this grief, and we can trust in Him until that time comes. There is no breakup, no loss, and no rejection from which God cannot and will not heal us.

Action Step

Ask a parent or an older, trusted believer to share with you how they have seen God bring healing from a past hurt in their own lives.

29

lie: I would be happy, if only I were more like _____

We can scroll on our phones and become envious of someone who has more followers than us. We can look around us at school and wish we were like the student who has more friends than us. The unhealthy habit of comparison enables us to look at those who seem happy and thriving and feel like we need to be like them. We can examine ourselves and believe that we need to change so that we can experience the happiness or successes others seem to be experiencing.

Comparison can lie to us and cause us to make assumptions that are not always true. We might think the girl on social media with the many followers has a great life, but we do not see the struggles that are not displayed online. We may assume that the student with lots of friends feels affirmed and well-liked, but we do not see the inward insecurities she battles. But comparison can also lie to us by leading us to believe that becoming like another person will ensure our happiness. And, while we can learn from others and make wise and healthy changes in our lives, changing ourselves to be like another person does not promise joy. In fact, it can lead to even further discouragement when we realize we still do not have what we desire, even after changing ourselves.

The desire to be like others causes us to devalue the person God created us to be. God has made each one of us intentionally, and who He has created us to be is not to be changed but celebrated. And, while God desires each one of us to develop in Christlikeness and walk in holiness, He does not want us to change the unique ways we have been designed. Our physical appearances, personalities, and skills were given to us by a good and intentional God. When we embrace these gifts and use them in God-glorifying ways, we will experience joy.

Ultimately, it is not being like others that will make us happy but being like Christ. Pursuing Christlikeness forms us more and more into the image of Jesus and causes us to become the holy people God created us to be. Being formed into the image of Christ leads to true joy because we are living as God intended and commands. Unless we imitate the walks of faithful believers, any other worldly imitation will keep us from pursuing Christlikeness. Instead of desiring to be like others, our greatest desire should be to be like Jesus.

In John 21:21–22, Peter looks at another disciple and inquires about his fate. Jesus responds by saying, "'If I want him to remain until I come … what is that to you? As for you, follow me.'" These verses teach us that we should be more consumed with following Jesus than with what other people do. This does not mean we cannot celebrate the successes of others or think about ways to care for and support others, but it does mean that our eyes should be fixed upon Jesus over anyone else. As we follow Jesus, we will learn to embrace how God made us and how He is using our unique qualities for His kingdom purposes.

Action Step

Consider who you are currently comparing yourself to and desiring to be like. Why do you want to be like this person? How can you reorient these desires to desire to be like Jesus instead?

30

Lie:

I messed up God's plan for me

99

Our relationship with Christ not only gives us true
affirmation but also heart transformation.

30

There are moments in which we can all feel as if our choices or failures have messed up God's plan. Perhaps you did not get into the college you wanted to go to, and now you don't know where to continue your education. Or maybe you quit a sport or hobby and believe that you have caused yourself to miss out on future opportunities or successes because of this decision. We can also feel as if we have messed up God's plans because of sinful choices we have made. Maybe you had sex outside of marriage, and now you are pregnant. Or perhaps you got caught using drugs or drinking underage, and now you have a mark on your record. These decisions might make us feel ashamed and afraid that our mistakes have ruined God's plans and purposes.

While sinful choices can complicate our lives and inhibit certain opportunities, nothing can ruin God's plans. One of the most comforting truths about God is that He is sovereign. In His sovereignty and providence, God orchestrates events according to His perfect will. This means that whatever God has ordained to happen will always come to pass. While God's sovereignty can be hard to grasp, the fact that God's plans will always succeed is incredibly encouraging. Because of God's sovereignty, we never have to worry that we have messed up God's plans. After all, to believe this lie is to believe that we have more power than the God of the universe. Thankfully, we do not have enough power to ruin God's plans, which is a reason to rejoice.

Another aspect of God's sovereignty is that He works through our sinful choices and mistakes. Even if we do something that is not pleasing to the Lord, we can be confident that He will still work through our situation to accomplish His purposes. If we doubt this to be true, we can remind ourselves of the story of Israel. God picked the people of Israel as His chosen people. He formed a covenant with them and promised to lead, guide, and form them into a thriving nation. But Israel did not listen to God's commands, and they soon turned away from Him to worship false gods. All throughout the Old Testament, we see how Israel failed in their end of their covenant with God and did not walk in His ways. Their disobedience and unrepentance ultimately led them to be ripped away from their land and placed into exile. But, even though Israel failed in their obedience to God, God was faithful to fulfill His covenant with His people and His plan of redemption. And ultimately, we know this to be true because of Christ.

Israel's unfaithfulness could not thwart God's plans, and our choices and failures cannot thwart God's plans. Yet this truth is not a license to do whatever we please. Instead, it should encourage us to keep seeking and walking in God's ways. As we remain obedient to God and His Word, we can be confident that we are following God's plans. Even if we make a detour or do not know if we are taking the right step, we can trust that God will redirect us and lead us down His path.

BECAUSE OF GOD'S SOVEREIGNTY, WE NEVER HAVE TO WORRY THAT WE HAVE MESSED UP GOD'S PLANS.

Action Step

Read Jeremiah 29:11 and Psalm 33:11, and then write these verses somewhere you will continually see them—whether that's on your bathroom mirror, in your planner, or on a sticky note. As you go throughout your day, ask the Lord to help you trust His plans and walk in His ways.

notes

BIBLIOGRAPHY

Henley, William Ernest. "Invictus." *Poetry Foundation*. The Poetry
Foundation. Accessed April 22, 2022. https://www.poetryfounda-
tion.org/poems/51642/invictus.

Thank you for studying
God's Word with us!

CONNECT WITH US
@THEDAILYGRACECO
@DAILYGRACEPODCAST

CONTACT US
INFO@THEDAILYGRACECO.COM

SHARE
#THEDAILYGRACECO

VISIT US ONLINE
WWW.THEDAILYGRACECO.COM

MORE DAILY GRACE
THE DAILY GRACE APP
DAILY GRACE PODCAST